Better Homes and Ga...

MAKE AHEAD and MICROWAVE

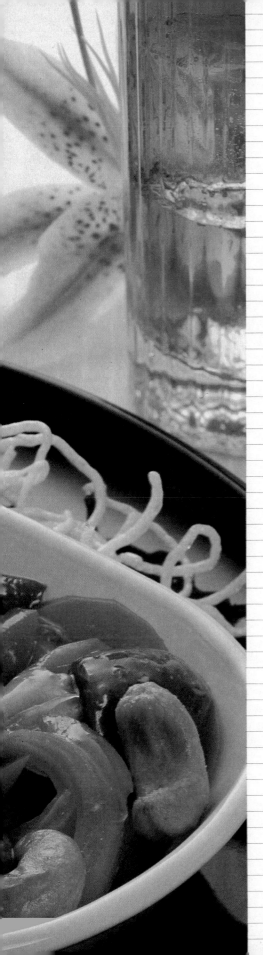

What's even better than an easy way to fix dinner? Two time-savers—the speed of the microwave oven and the convenience of making food ahead—used as a team.

Begin by preparing one of our recipes in your microwave oven when you have time. Then chill the dish to serve the next day or freeze it to serve weeks later. To have dinner in minutes, just pop the ready-made dish into your microwave oven for the time specified.

To make this booklet as useful as possible, we tested all of the recipes in both high-wattage (600- to 700-watt) ovens and low-wattage (400- to 550-watt) ovens. If no low-wattage tip is given, then the directions will work equally well in either type of oven. If the cooking time or power setting in the low-wattage oven was different from that in the high-wattage oven, you'll find the low-wattage directions listed immediately after the main recipe or reheating directions.

Whether you need a quick main dish for a group, a speedy entrée for one, or a hurry-up side dish or dessert, you'll find a recipe in *Make Ahead and Microwave* to fit your busy schedule.

Having Cashew Chicken and
Peach Coffee Cake, left, (see
recipes, pages 15 and 21) in the
freezer or the refrigerator is as
handy as money in the bank.
Make a quick withdrawal when
you need a no-fuss meal.

Lemon Beef Stroganoff

For a fresh look, garnish each serving with a sprig of basil.

2 **pounds beef round steak,
   partially frozen**
4 **medium carrots, thinly sliced
   (2 cups)**
4 **stalks celery, sliced (2 cups)**
1 **medium onion, chopped
   (½ cup)**
1 **clove garlic, minced**
1 **10½-ounce can condensed
   beef broth**
1 **4½-ounce jar sliced
   mushrooms, drained**
¼ **cup red wine vinegar**
1 **teaspoon dried basil, crushed**
1 **teaspoon finely shredded
   lemon peel**
½ **teaspoon paprika**
⅛ **teaspoon pepper**
....
¼ **cup all-purpose flour**
1 **cup dairy sour cream**
   Hot cooked fettuccine
   or **noodles**

■ Slice meat across grain into bite-size strips. In a 3-quart casserole cook meat, covered, on 100% power (high) for 8 to 10 minutes or till no pink remains, stirring twice. Drain.

■ Add carrots, celery, onion, and garlic to meat. Stir in broth, mushrooms, vinegar, dried basil, lemon peel, paprika, and pepper. Cook, covered, on high for 5 minutes; stir. Cook on 70% power (medium-high) for 18 to 22 minutes or till meat is just tender, stirring every 5 minutes. Divide mixture between two 4-cup airtight containers. Seal and label. Chill or freeze. Makes 2 portions, 4 servings each.

Low-wattage oven: For *meat strips,* cook on high for 12 to 15 minutes. For *meat-and-vegetable mixture,* cook on high for 20 to 25 minutes total, stirring every 5 minutes.

REHEAT: CHILLED	REHEAT: FROZEN

In a 2-quart casserole cook 1 chilled portion, covered, on 100% power (high) for 8 to 10 minutes or till heated through, stirring once. Stir *2 tablespoons* flour into *½ cup* sour cream; stir into meat mixture. Cook, uncovered, on high for 2 to 4 minutes or till thickened and bubbly, stirring every minute. Cook on high for 30 seconds more. Serve over fettuccine.

Low-wattage oven: For *chilled portion,* cook on high for 10 to 13 minutes. For *meat mixture with sour cream,* cook on high for 4 to 6 minutes.

In a 2-quart casserole cook 1 frozen portion, covered, on 70% power (medium-high) for 16 to 20 minutes or till heated through, stirring 3 times. Stir *2 tablespoons* flour into *½ cup* sour cream; stir into meat mixture. Cook, uncovered, on 100% power (high) for 2 to 4 minutes or till thickened and bubbly, stirring every minute. Cook on high for 30 seconds more. Serve over fettuccine.

Low-wattage oven: For *frozen portion,* cook on high for 17 to 20 minutes. For *meat mixture with sour cream,* cook on high 4 to 6 minutes.

Oriental Beef

Round out the menu by cutting wedges of Chinese cabbage or lettuce for salads and scooping sherbet for dessert.

1 pound ground beef
   or ground pork
1 clove garlic, minced
½ cup cold water
3 tablespoons soy sauce
1 tablespoon quick-cooking
   tapioca
¼ teaspoon ground ginger
⅛ teaspoon ground red pepper
2 cups loose-pack frozen
   broccoli, cauliflower,
   and carrots
1 medium green pepper,
   cut into strips
1 8-ounce can sliced
   water chestnuts, drained
¾ cup water
½ cup quick-cooking rice

■ In a 1½-quart casserole cook ground beef or pork and garlic, covered, on 100% power (high) for 4 to 6 minutes or till no pink remains, stirring once. Drain off fat.

■ Combine ½ cup cold water, soy sauce, tapioca, ginger, and red pepper; stir into meat. Cook, uncovered, on high for 3 to 5 minutes or till thickened and bubbly, stirring twice. Stir in frozen vegetables, green pepper, water chestnuts, ¾ cup water, and *uncooked* rice. Transfer to a 1½-quart airtight container. Seal and label. Chill or freeze. Makes 4 servings.

REHEAT: CHILLED	REHEAT: FROZEN

▨ In a 1½-quart casserole cook chilled meat mixture, covered, on 100% power (high) for 13 to 16 minutes or till vegetables and rice are tender, stirring twice.
Low-wattage oven: Cook on high for 17 to 20 minutes.

▨ In a 1½-quart casserole cook frozen meat mixture, covered, on 70% power (medium-high) for 25 to 30 minutes or till vegetables and rice are tender, stirring twice to break mixture apart.
Low-wattage oven: Cook on high for 25 to 30 minutes.

Creamy Pork Casserole

When you're in a hurry, substitute one 16-ounce package of frozen cut green beans for the fresh green beans and cook them according to the package's microwave directions.

1 pound green beans, cut
    into 1-inch pieces
2 tablespoons water
1½ pounds boneless pork,
    partially frozen
¼ cup chopped onion
1 10¾-ounce can condensed
    cream of celery soup
1 8-ounce carton dairy
    sour cream
⅔ cup milk
½ cup shredded carrot
1 cup herb-seasoned
    stuffing mix

. . . .

2 tablespoons butter
    or margarine
1 cup herb-seasoned
    stuffing mix

■ In a 2-quart casserole combine beans and water. Cook, covered, on 100% power (high) for 9 to 11 minutes or till just crisp-tender, stirring once. Drain in a colander; set aside.

■ Slice pork across grain into bite-size strips. In the same casserole cook pork and onion, covered, on high for 6 to 8 minutes or till no pink remains in meat and onion is tender, stirring once. Drain off juices. Stir cooked beans, celery soup, sour cream, milk, and carrot into meat. Fold in 1 cup stuffing mix. Transfer mixture to a 2-quart airtight container. Seal and label. Chill or freeze. Makes 6 servings.
Low-wattage oven: For *beans,* cook on high for 13 to 16 minutes. For *pork,* cook on high for 8 to 10 minutes.

REHEAT: CHILLED	REHEAT: FROZEN

■ In a microwave-safe bowl cook butter or margarine, uncovered, on 100% power (high) for 30 seconds or till melted. Add 1 cup stuffing mix. Toss to coat. Set aside.

In a 2-quart casserole cook chilled mixture, covered, on 70% power (medium-high) for 20 to 25 minutes or till hot, stirring twice. Top with crumb mixture. Cook, uncovered, on medium-high for 1 minute more.
Low-wattage oven: For *chilled mixture,* cook on high for 17 to 20 minutes. Cook with crumb mixture, uncovered, on high for 1 minute more.

■ In a microwave-safe bowl cook butter or margarine, uncovered, on 100% power (high) for 30 seconds or till melted. Add 1 cup stuffing mix. Toss to coat. Set aside.

In a 2-quart casserole cook frozen mixture, covered, on 70% power (medium-high) for 40 to 45 minutes or till heated through, stirring every 10 minutes. Top with the crumb mixture. Cook, uncovered, on medium-high for 1 minute more.
Low-wattage oven: For *frozen mixture,* cook on high for 40 to 45 minutes. Cook with crumb mixture, uncovered, on high for 1 minute more.

7

Creole-Style Chicken And Shrimp

Serve this peppy Louisiana-style dish with French bread or hard rolls, à la New Orleans. (Also pictured on the cover.)

1 medium green pepper, chopped (1 cup)
1 medium onion, chopped (½ cup)
2 cloves garlic, minced
1 tablespoon butter *or* margarine
1 16-ounce can tomatoes, cut up
1 cup frozen diced cooked chicken
4 ounces frozen cooked shrimp (about 1 cup)
½ of a 6-ounce can (⅓ cup) tomato paste
1 teaspoon sugar
½ teaspoon dried thyme, crushed
½ teaspoon chili powder
¼ teaspoon salt
¼ teaspoon pepper
Several dashes bottled hot pepper sauce
....
Hot cooked rice

■ In a 2-quart casserole combine green pepper, onion, garlic, and butter or margarine. Cook, covered, on 100% power (high) for 2 to 3 minutes or till onion is tender.

■ Stir in *undrained* tomatoes, chicken, shrimp, tomato paste, sugar, thyme, chili powder, salt, pepper, and hot pepper sauce. Transfer mixture to a 1½-quart airtight container. Seal and label. Chill or freeze. Makes 4 servings.
Low-wattage oven: Cook on high for 3 to 5 minutes.

REHEAT: CHILLED	REHEAT: FROZEN

■ In a 2-quart casserole cook chilled mixture, covered, on 100% power (high) for 9 to 11 minutes or till heated through, stirring twice. Serve over hot cooked rice.
Low-wattage oven: Cook on high for 13 to 16 minutes.

■ In a 2-quart casserole cook frozen mixture, covered, on 100% power (high) for 15 to 18 minutes or till heated through, stirring twice. Serve over hot cooked rice.
Low-wattage oven: Cook on high for 23 to 28 minutes.

Tomato-Sauce Base

One easy sauce makes six meals with three different flavors.

1 cup shredded carrot
1 cup chopped onion
½ cup chopped green pepper
¼ cup chopped celery
3 cloves garlic, minced
1 tablespoon cooking oil
2 15-ounce cans tomato sauce·
3 6-ounce cans tomato paste

■ In a 3-quart casserole combine carrot, onion, green pepper, celery, garlic, and cooking oil. Cook, covered, on 100% power (high) for 6 to 8 minutes or till onion is tender, stirring once. Stir in tomato sauce and tomato paste. Divide mixture into three 2-cup portions. Use in the following recipes: Spaghetti and Meatballs (below) and Chunky Chili and Sausage-Macaroni Bake (opposite). **Low-wattage oven:** Cook on high for 8 to 10 minutes.

Spaghetti and Meatballs

While the sauce reheats in the microwave oven, cook the spaghetti on the range.

1 beaten egg
¾ cup soft bread crumbs (1 slice)
¼ cup finely chopped onion
2 tablespoons milk
½ teaspoon salt
1 pound ground beef
1 2-cup portion Tomato-
   Sauce Base
2 4-ounce cans sliced
   mushrooms, drained
¼ cup dry red wine
1 teaspoon sugar
1 teaspoon dried oregano,
   crushed
1 teaspoon dried basil, crushed
½ teaspoon salt
½ teaspoon dried thyme, crushed
....
½ cup water
   Hot cooked spaghetti

■ In a medium mixing bowl combine egg, crumbs, onion, milk, and ½ teaspoon salt. Add ground beef; mix well. Shape into twenty-four 1-inch meatballs. Place meatballs in an 8x8x2-inch baking dish. Cover with waxed paper. Cook on 100% power (high) for 6 to 9 minutes or till no pink remains, turning meatballs over and rearranging once. Drain off fat. In a bowl stir together sauce base, mushrooms, wine, sugar, oregano, basil, ½ teaspoon salt, and thyme. Divide meatballs and sauce between two 3-cup airtight containers. Seal and label. Chill or freeze. Makes 2 portions, 2 or 3 servings each.

REHEAT: CHILLED
▥ In a 1½-quart casserole combine 1 chilled portion and ¼ *cup* water. Cook, covered, on 100% power (high) for 8 to 10 minutes or till hot, stirring twice. Serve over spaghetti. **Low-wattage oven:** Cook on high for 10 to 12 minutes.

REHEAT: FROZEN
▥ In a 1½-quart casserole cook 1 frozen portion, covered, on 100% power (high) 10 to 13 minutes or till thawed, stirring gently twice. Add ¼ *cup* water. Cook, covered, on high 5 to 7 minutes or till hot, stirring 3 times. Serve over spaghetti.

10

Chunky Chili

Corn adds a splash of gold.

1 pound ground beef
1 2-cup portion Tomato-
    Sauce Base
2 tablespoons chili powder
1 teaspoon dry mustard
½ teaspoon salt
    Several dashes bottled hot
    pepper sauce (optional)
1 15½-ounce can red
    kidney beans
1 10-ounce package frozen
    whole kernel corn

■ In a 1½-quart casserole crumble beef. Cook, covered, on 100% power (high) 4 to 6 minutes or till no pink remains, stirring once. Drain. Add sauce base, chili powder, mustard, salt, and pepper sauce, if desired. Cook, uncovered, on high for 3 to 5 minutes or till bubbly. Add *undrained* beans and corn. Spoon into two 1-quart airtight containers. Seal and label. Chill or freeze. Makes 2 portions, 3 servings each.

REHEAT: CHILLED
▨ In a 1½-quart casserole place 1 chilled portion and ¾ cup *water*. Cook, covered, on 100% power (high) for 8 to 10 minutes or till hot, stirring twice.
Low-wattage oven: Cook on high for 11 to 13 minutes.

REHEAT: FROZEN
▨ In a 1½-quart casserole place 1 frozen portion and ¾ cup *hot water*. Cook, covered, on 100% power (high) for 16 to 18 minutes or till hot, stirring 3 times.
Low-wattage oven: Cook on high for 23 to 28 minutes.

Sausage-Macaroni Bake

1 pound bulk Italian sausage
1 2-cup portion Tomato-
    Sauce Base
1 10-ounce package frozen peas
½ cup elbow macaroni, cooked
    and drained
¾ cup water
1 teaspoon chili powder
⅛ teaspoon pepper
....
4 slices American cheese, cut
    into triangles

■ In a 2-quart casserole crumble sausage. Cook sausage, covered, on 100% power (high) for 6 to 8 minutes or till juices run clear, stirring once. Drain off fat. Stir in sauce base, peas, cooked macaroni, water, chili powder, and pepper. Divide mixture between two 1-quart airtight containers. Seal and label. Chill or freeze. Makes 2 portions, 3 servings each.
Low-wattage oven: Cook on high for 8 to 10 minutes.

REHEAT: CHILLED
▨ In a 1½-quart casserole cook 1 chilled portion, covered, on 100% power (high) 8 to 10 minutes or till hot, stirring twice. Arrange *2 slices* cheese atop. Let stand, covered, 3 minutes.
Low-wattage oven: Cook on high for 11 to 14 minutes.

REHEAT: FROZEN
▨ In a 1½-quart casserole cook 1 frozen portion, covered, on 70% power (medium-high) for 15 to 18 minutes or till hot, stirring twice. Arrange *2 slices* cheese atop mixture. Let stand, covered, for 3 minutes to melt cheese.
Low-wattage oven: Cook on high for 15 to 18 minutes.

Tamale Pie

1¼ cups water
½ cup yellow cornmeal
2 teaspoons butter *or* margarine
¼ teaspoon salt
¼ teaspoon ground cumin
⅛ teaspoon pepper
1 pound ground beef
1 large onion, chopped (1 cup)
1 medium green *or* red sweet pepper, chopped (1 cup)
1 medium carrot, quartered and sliced (½ cup)
1 clove garlic, minced
2 teaspoons chili powder
1 15-ounce can tomato sauce
1 12-ounce can whole kernel corn, drained
1 4-ounce can diced green chili peppers, drained
½ cup sliced pitted ripe olives

Use cookie cutters to cut the cornmeal mixture into fun shapes.

■ In a 1½-quart casserole combine water, cornmeal, butter, salt, cumin, and pepper. Cook, uncovered, on 100% power (high) for 4 to 6 minutes or till very thick, stirring every minute. Spread mixture on waxed paper into an 8-inch square about ¼ inch thick. Chill. Cut into 18 small shapes. Place shapes on a baking sheet in a single layer. Cover; chill or freeze till firm. Store frozen shapes in a sealed freezer bag.

■ In a 2-quart casserole combine beef, onion, green pepper, carrot, garlic, and chili powder. Cook, covered, on high 7 to 9 minutes or till no pink remains; stir once. Drain. Stir in tomato sauce, corn, chili peppers, and olives. Spoon mixture into 6 casseroles. Seal and label. Chill or freeze. Serves 6.
Low-wattage oven: For *cornmeal mixture,* cook on high for 6 to 8 minutes. For *beef mixture,* cook on high 9 to 11 minutes.

REHEAT: CHILLED	REHEAT: FROZEN

FOR 1 SERVING
Cook 1 chilled casserole, covered, on 100% power (high) for 3 to 4 minutes or till hot, stirring once. Top with 3 cornmeal shapes. Cook, uncovered, on high for 1 to 2 minutes more or till shapes are heated through.

FOR 1 SERVING
Cook 1 casserole, covered, on 70% power (medium-high) 2 minutes; stir. Add 3 shapes. Cook on medium-high for 5 to 7 minutes or till hot.
Low-wattage oven: Cook on high for 3 minutes, then with shapes for 5 to 7 minutes.

FOR 2 SERVINGS
Cook 2 chilled casseroles, covered, on 100% power (high) for 5 to 6 minutes or till hot, stirring once. Top *each* casserole with 3 cornmeal shapes. Cook, uncovered, on high for 2 to 3 minutes more or till shapes are heated through.

FOR 2 SERVINGS
Cook 2 casseroles, covered, on 70% power (medium-high) for 4 minutes; stir once. Top *each* with 3 cornmeal shapes. Cook on medium-high for 9 to 12 minutes or till hot.
Low-wattage oven: Cook on high for 4 minutes, then with shapes for 9 to 12 minutes.

Ham-Stuffed Sweet Potatoes

All the flavors of a holiday meal in one dish.

4 medium sweet potatoes
   (6 to 8 ounces each)
¼ cup butter *or* margarine
2 cups diced fully cooked ham
⅓ cup cranberry-orange sauce
2 tablespoons brown sugar
¼ teaspoon salt

■ Scrub potatoes. Prick several times with a fork. Arrange on a microwave-safe plate. Cook, uncovered, on 100% power (high) for 14 to 17 minutes or till tender, rearranging and turning potatoes over once. Let stand for 5 minutes.

■ Cut a lengthwise slice from the top of each potato. Remove the skin from top slices and put the pulp into a small mixer bowl. Scoop the pulp from each potato, leaving a ½-inch-thick shell. Add pulp to the mixer bowl. Set shells aside. Add butter or margarine to potato pulp. Mash potato pulp. Stir in diced ham, cranberry-orange sauce, brown sugar, and salt. Spoon *one-fourth* of the mixture into *each* potato shell. Wrap each potato in heavy-duty foil or place all in an airtight container. Seal and label. Chill or freeze. Makes 4 servings.
Low-wattage oven: Cook on high for 20 to 23 minutes.

REHEAT: CHILLED	REHEAT: FROZEN

FOR 1 SERVING
Unwrap 1 chilled potato and place on a microwave-safe plate. Cook, uncovered, on 100% power (high) for 3 to 5 minutes or till heated through. Let stand 5 minutes.
Low-wattage oven: Cook on high for 5 to 7 minutes.

FOR 1 SERVING
Unwrap 1 frozen potato and place on a microwave-safe plate. Cook, uncovered, on 70% power (medium-high) for 8 to 10 minutes or till hot. Let stand 5 minutes.
Low-wattage oven: Cook on high for 6 to 8 minutes.

FOR 2 SERVINGS
Unwrap 2 chilled potatoes and place on a microwave-safe plate. Cook, uncovered, on 100% power (high) for 5 to 7 minutes or till heated through. Let stand 5 minutes.
Low-wattage oven: Cook on high for 8 to 10 minutes.

FOR 2 SERVINGS
Unwrap 2 frozen potatoes and place on a microwave-safe plate. Cook, uncovered, on 70% power (medium-high) for 12 to 15 minutes or till hot. Let stand 5 minutes.
Low-wattage oven: Cook on high for 11 to 14 minutes.

Cashew Chicken

Serve with fried bean threads. You'll find bean threads at Oriental food stores or large supermarkets. (Pictured on page 2.)

½ cup water
¼ cup soy sauce
¼ cup dry sherry
1 tablespoon quick-cooking tapioca
1 teaspoon sugar
½ teaspoon grated fresh gingerroot *or* ¼ teaspoon ground ginger
¼ teaspoon crushed red pepper
2 medium carrots, thinly bias-sliced
1 medium green pepper, cut into ¾-inch pieces
1 small onion, cut into wedges
¼ cup water
2 whole medium chicken breasts, skinned, boned, and cut into 1-inch pieces
....
½ cup cashews

■ In a 2-cup measure stir together ½ cup water, soy sauce, sherry, tapioca, sugar, gingerroot, and red pepper. Set aside. In a 1½-quart casserole combine carrots, green pepper, onion, and ¼ cup water. Cook, covered, on 100% power (high) for 4 to 6 minutes or till just tender. Drain; set aside. In the same casserole cook chicken, covered, on high for 4 to 6 minutes or till no pink remains, stirring once. Drain.

■ Stir soy mixture. Cook, uncovered, on high for 2 to 4 minutes or till bubbly, stirring every minute. Cook for 1 minute more. Stir soy mixture and vegetables into chicken. Spoon mixture into 4 individual casseroles. Seal and label. Chill or freeze. Makes 4 servings.
Low-wattage oven: For *carrot mixture,* cook on high for 6 to 8 minutes.

REHEAT: CHILLED	REHEAT: FROZEN

FOR 1 SERVING
■ Cook 1 chilled casserole, covered, on 100% power (high) for 2 to 4 minutes or till heated through, stirring once. Sprinkle *2 tablespoons* cashews atop casserole.
Low-wattage oven: Cook on high for 3 to 5 minutes.

FOR 1 SERVING
■ Cook 1 frozen casserole, covered, on 70% power (medium-high) for 5 to 7 minutes or till hot, stirring once. Sprinkle with *2 tablespoons* cashews.
Low-wattage oven: Cook on high for 5 to 7 minutes.

FOR 2 SERVINGS
■ Cook 2 chilled casseroles, covered, on 100% power (high) for 5 to 7 minutes or till heated through, stirring once. Sprinkle *2 tablespoons* cashews atop *each* casserole.
Low-wattage oven: Cook on high for 6 to 8 minutes.

FOR 2 SERVINGS
■ Cook 2 frozen casseroles, covered, on 70% power (medium-high) for 9 to 11 minutes or till hot, stirring once. Sprinkle *2 tablespoons* cashews atop *each* casserole.
Low-wattage oven: Cook on high for 9 to 11 minutes.

15

Broccoli au Gratin

This easy side dish goes great with salmon, turkey, or ham.

1 pound broccoli, cut into
½-inch pieces (about
4 cups)
¼ cup water
1 cup milk
2 tablespoons cornstarch
⅛ teaspoon pepper
1 cup shredded American
cheese (4 ounces)
....
1 tablespoon butter *or*
margarine
¼ cup fine dry bread crumbs

■ In a 1½-quart casserole combine broccoli and water. Cook, covered, on 100% power (high) for 5 to 7 minutes or till tender, stirring once. Drain in a colander; set aside.

■ For sauce, in the same casserole combine milk, cornstarch, and pepper. Cook, uncovered, on high for 3 to 5 minutes or till thickened and bubbly, stirring every minute. Add shredded cheese; stir till melted. Stir in broccoli. Transfer mixture to a 1-quart airtight container. Seal and label. Chill or freeze. Makes 6 servings.
Low-wattage oven: For *broccoli and water,* cook on high for 7 to 9 minutes.

REHEAT: CHILLED	REHEAT: FROZEN

■ In a small microwave-safe bowl cook butter or margarine, uncovered, on 100% power (high) for 30 to 40 seconds or till melted. Stir in bread crumbs and set aside.

In a 1½-quart casserole cook chilled broccoli mixture, covered, on high for 9 to 11 minutes or till heated through, stirring twice. Sprinkle buttered crumbs over broccoli mixture.
Low-wattage oven: For *broccoli mixture,* cook on high for 12 to 14 minutes.

■ In a small microwave-safe bowl cook butter or margarine, uncovered, on 100% power (high) for 30 to 40 seconds or till melted. Stir in bread crumbs and set aside.

In a 1½-quart casserole cook frozen broccoli mixture, covered, on 70% power (medium-high) for 17 to 20 minutes or till heated through, stirring twice. Sprinkle buttered crumbs over broccoli mixture.
Low-wattage oven: For *broccoli mixture,* cook on high for 20 to 25 minutes.

Stuffed Potatoes Florentine

Stockpile a supply of these stuffed potatoes to accompany ham or steak dinners.

4 medium baking potatoes
(4 to 6 ounces each)
1 10-ounce package frozen
chopped spinach
½ cup sour cream dip
with onion
2 tablespoons butter *or*
margarine
1 tablespoon milk
¼ teaspoon pepper
½ cup shredded cheddar
cheese (2 ounces)
....

Shredded cheddar cheese
(optional)

■ Scrub potatoes. Prick several times with a fork. Arrange potatoes on a microwave-safe plate. Cook, uncovered, on 100% power (high) for 14 to 17 minutes or till tender, rearranging and turning potatoes over once. Let stand for 5 minutes. In a 1½-quart casserole cook spinach, covered, on high for 5 to 7 minutes or till tender, stirring once. Drain well, squeezing out excess liquid.

■ Cut a lengthwise slice from the top of each potato. Remove the skin from top slices and put the pulp into a small mixer bowl. Scoop pulp from each potato, leaving a ¼-inch-thick shell. Add pulp to the mixer bowl. Set shells aside.

■ Add dip, butter or margarine, milk, and pepper to potato pulp. Beat with an electric mixer on medium speed till smooth. Stir in spinach and ½ cup cheese. Spoon *one-fourth* of the potato mixture into *each* potato shell. Wrap each potato in heavy-duty foil or place potatoes in an airtight container. Seal and label. Chill or freeze. Makes 4 servings.
Low-wattage oven: For *potatoes,* cook on high for 19 to 22 minutes. For *spinach,* cook on high for 7 to 9 minutes.

REHEAT: CHILLED	REHEAT: FROZEN

■ Unwrap 4 chilled potatoes and place in an 8x8x2-inch baking dish. Cover with waxed paper. Cook on 70% power (medium-high) for 11 to 14 minutes or till heated through, turning dish and rearranging potatoes once. If desired, sprinkle additional cheese on potatoes. Let stand, covered, for 5 minutes.
Low-wattage oven: Cook on high for 13 to 16 minutes.

■ Unwrap 4 frozen potatoes and place in an 8x8x2-inch baking dish. Cover with waxed paper. Cook on 70% power (medium-high) for 17 to 20 minutes or till heated through, turning dish and rearranging potatoes twice. If desired, sprinkle additional cheese on potatoes. Let stand, covered, for 5 minutes.
Low-wattage oven: Cook on high for 15 to 18 minutes.

French Onion Soup

Invite friends over after the theater or a game for French Onion Soup, hearty red wine, and crusty French bread.

2 large onions, thinly sliced
1 clove garlic, minced
2 tablespoons butter *or* margarine
2 10½-ounce cans condensed beef broth

....

1⅓ cups water
4 ½-inch-thick slices French bread, toasted
4 slices Swiss *or* Gruyère cheese
   Grated Parmesan cheese

■ In a 2-quart casserole combine onion, garlic, and butter or margarine. Cook, covered, on 100% power (high) for 10 to 13 minutes or till onion is very tender, stirring once. Stir in beef broth. Pour into a 1½-quart airtight container. Seal and label. Chill or freeze. Makes 4 servings.
Low-wattage oven: Cook on high for 15 to 18 minutes.

REHEAT: CHILLED	REHEAT: FROZEN

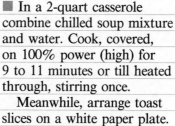

■ In a 2-quart casserole combine chilled soup mixture and water. Cook, covered, on 100% power (high) for 9 to 11 minutes or till heated through, stirring once.

Meanwhile, arrange toast slices on a white paper plate. Top each toast slice with a slice of Swiss or Gruyère cheese; sprinkle with Parmesan cheese. Cook, uncovered, on high for 1 minute or till cheese melts, rearranging toast slices once. Ladle hot soup into bowls. Top with toast slices.
Low-wattage oven: For *soup,* cook on high for 13 to 16 minutes.

■ In a 2-quart casserole combine frozen soup mixture and water. Cook, covered, on 70% power (medium-high) for 20 to 25 minutes or till heated through, stirring 3 times.

Meanwhile, arrange toast slices on a white paper plate. Top toast slices with Swiss or Gruyère cheese; sprinkle with Parmesan cheese. Cook, uncovered, on 100% power (high) for 1 minute or till cheese melts, rearranging toast slices once. Ladle hot soup into bowls. Top with toast slices.
Low-wattage oven: For *soup,* cook on high for 20 to 25 minutes.

Cinnamon-Apple Coffee Cake

¼ cup finely chopped nuts
¼ cup packed brown sugar
½ teaspoon ground cinnamon
1 cup all-purpose flour
1 teaspoon baking powder
¼ teaspoon baking soda
¼ cup shortening
½ cup sugar
1 egg
½ teaspoon vanilla
½ cup dairy sour cream
¾ cup finely chopped
    peeled apple

The nut topping gives this buttery cake color and crunch.

■ Grease a 6½-cup microwave-safe ring mold. In a small bowl combine nuts, brown sugar, and cinnamon. Sprinkle nut mixture over bottom and sides of ring mold. Set aside.

■ In a bowl combine flour, baking powder, and baking soda. In a small mixer bowl beat shortening with an electric mixer on medium speed for 30 seconds. Add sugar and beat till fluffy. Add egg and vanilla; beat well. Add flour mixture and sour cream alternately to beaten mixture. Fold in chopped apple. Spread batter evenly in the prepared dish.

■ Cook, uncovered, on 50% power (medium) for 9 minutes, giving the dish a quarter-turn every 3 minutes. If not done, cook on 100% power (high) for 30 seconds to 2 minutes more or till surface is nearly dry.

■ Cool coffee cake in the dish on a wire rack for 10 minutes. To loosen cake, run a narrow metal spatula around edges. Invert onto a wire rack and remove the dish. Spread any leftover topping in the dish onto cake. Cool completely. Wrap cake in moisture- and vaporproof wrap. Seal, label, and freeze. Makes 8 servings.
Low-wattage oven: Cook on high for 6 to 8 minutes total or till surface of cake is nearly dry, giving the dish a quarter-turn every 2 minutes.

REHEAT: FROZEN

■ Unwrap coffee cake; place on a microwave-safe plate. Cook, uncovered, on 30% power (medium-low) for 6 to 8 minutes or till warm, turning dish once.
Low-wattage oven: Cook on 30% power (defrost) for 6 to 8 minutes.

Peach Coffee Cake

Pass the hot peach-orange sauce to drizzle over the coffee cake. (Pictured on page 2.)

2 tablespoons finely crushed
    graham crackers (1 *or*
    2 squares)
1½ cups all-purpose flour
½ cup sugar
1 teaspoon baking powder
½ cup butter *or* margarine
1 beaten egg
⅔ cup milk
½ cup fresh *or* frozen
    chopped peaches
¼ cup orange marmalade
½ teaspoon cornstarch

■ Grease a 6½-cup microwave-safe ring mold; coat with crushed crackers. In a medium bowl combine flour, sugar, and baking powder. Cut in butter till crumbly. Combine egg and milk. Add to flour mixture; stir till moistened. Spread batter evenly in prepared dish. In a 1-cup measure combine peaches and marmalade; spoon *¼ cup* mixture over batter.

■ Cook cake, uncovered, on 50% power (medium) for 9 minutes, giving dish a quarter-turn every 3 minutes. If not done, cook on 100% power (high) for 30 seconds to 2 minutes more or till surface is nearly dry. Cool on a wire rack for 10 minutes. Run a narrow metal spatula around edges. Invert onto a wire rack. Remove dish. Cool completely. Wrap cake in moisture- and vaporproof wrap. Seal, label, and freeze.

■ Stir cornstarch into remaining peach mixture. Cook, uncovered, on high for 1 to 2 minutes or till thickened and bubbly, stirring once. Pour into a 1-cup airtight container. Seal, label, and freeze. Makes 8 servings.
Low-wattage oven: For *cake,* cook on high for 8 to 10 minutes total, turning dish every 3 minutes. For *peach mixture,* cook on high for 3 to 4 minutes.

REHEAT: FROZEN

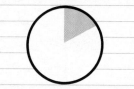

■ In a 1-cup measure cook peach mixture, uncovered, on 100% power (high) for 1 to 2 minutes or till hot, stirring once. Unwrap cake; place on a microwave-safe plate. Cook on 30% power (medium-low) for 9 to 12 minutes or till warm, turning once.
Low-wattage oven: For *cake,* cook on 30% power (defrost) for 11 to 13 minutes.

21

Cherry Dessert Topping

Each bite of fruit bursts with spicy sherry flavor.

1 16-ounce can pitted dark
   sweet cherries
1½ cups cranberry juice cocktail
5 inches stick cinnamon
2 ½-inch-thick slices fresh
   gingerroot
6 whole cloves
½ cup orange juice
2 tablespoons quick-cooking
   tapioca
1 6-ounce package mixed dried
   fruit bits
⅓ cup cream sherry
....
   Vanilla ice cream

■ Drain cherries, reserving syrup. Set cherries aside. In a 1½-quart casserole combine reserved syrup, cranberry juice, cinnamon, gingerroot, and cloves. Cook juice mixture, uncovered, on 100% power (high) for 6 to 8 minutes or till boiling, stirring once. Cook, covered, on 50% power (medium) for 10 minutes.

■ Meanwhile, in a small bowl combine orange juice and tapioca. Let stand for 5 minutes. Using a slotted spoon, remove cinnamon, gingerroot, and cloves from hot juice mixture. Add tapioca mixture and dried fruit to hot juice mixture. Cook, uncovered, on 100% power (high) for 4 to 6 minutes or till thickened and bubbly, stirring twice.

■ Add cherries and sherry. Divide mixture among four 1-cup airtight containers. Seal and label. Chill or freeze. Makes 4 portions, 4 servings each.
Low-wattage oven: For *juice mixture,* cook on high for 11 to 14 minutes or till boiling. Then cook, covered, on 30% power (defrost) for 12 minutes. For *juice mixture with tapioca and dried fruit,* cook, uncovered, on high for 7 to 9 minutes or till thickened and bubbly, stirring twice.

REHEAT: CHILLED	REHEAT: FROZEN
■ In a 1-quart casserole cook 1 chilled portion, uncovered, on 100% power (high) for 2 to 3 minutes or till hot, stirring once. Serve over vanilla ice cream. **Low-wattage oven:** Cook on high for 3 to 5 minutes.	■ In a 1-quart casserole cook 1 frozen portion, uncovered, on 100% power (high) for 3 to 5 minutes or till hot, stirring once. Serve over vanilla ice cream. **Low-wattage oven:** Cook on high for 5 to 7 minutes.

INDEX

Beef
    Chunky Chili, 11
    Lemon Beef Stroganoff, 4
    Oriental Beef, 6
    Spaghetti and Meatballs, 10
    Tamale Pie, 12
Broccoli au Gratin, 17
Cake
    Cinnamon-Apple Coffee
      Cake, 20
    Peach Coffee Cake, 21
Cashew Chicken, 15
Cherry Dessert Topping, 22
Chicken
    Cashew Chicken, 15
    Creole-Style Chicken and
      Shrimp, 9
Chunky Chili, 11
Cinnamon-Apple Coffee
    Cake, 20
Creamy Pork Casserole, 7
Creole-Style Chicken and
    Shrimp, 9
French Onion Soup, 19
Ham-Stuffed Sweet
    Potatoes, 14
Lemon Beef Stroganoff, 4
Oriental Beef, 6
Peach Coffee Cake, 21
Pork
    Creamy Pork Casserole, 7
    Ham-Stuffed Sweet
      Potatoes, 14
    Sausage-Macaroni Bake, 11
Potatoes
    Ham-Stuffed Sweet
      Potatoes, 14
    Stuffed Potatoes
      Florentine, 18
Sausage-Macaroni Bake, 11
Shrimp, Creole-Style Chicken
    and, 9
Soup, French Onion, 19
Spaghetti and Meatballs, 10
Stuffed Potatoes Florentine, 18
Tamale Pie, 12
Tomato-Sauce Base, 10

TIPS

Choosing the Right Dish

The shape and size of your dish can affect how evenly and fast foods cook in your microwave oven. For best results, use the shape and size dish called for in the recipe.

Changing the shape of the dish may cause some parts of your food to cook before others. Using another size dish may not allow space for the food to bubble or for you to stir the food.

Use nonmetallic dishes made of glass ceramic, oven-tempered glass, or heat-resistant glass. You also may use plastic dishes specially designed for microwave cooking. Look for cookware that is labeled safe for microwave use, either on the package or the dish.

Storing Make-Ahead Dishes

Your make-ahead recipes will taste just like fresh if you chill or freeze them properly.

Chill food in the refrigerator when you are going to serve it within 24 hours. Just cover the dish tightly and chill quickly.

Freeze food you want to keep longer than 24 hours. To store, place or wrap the food in airtight packaging, such as freezer containers, freezer paper, or heavy-duty foil. When you close the container or wrap, press out as much air as possible, then seal tightly.

Even the best memories fail, so label your package with the recipe title, number of servings, date frozen, and directions for reheating.

Plan to eat your frozen dish within 3 to 6 months for the best flavor and texture.